Rose Philippine Duchesne

A Dreamer and a Missionary

1769–1852
Born in Grenoble, France
Came to America in 1818
Feast Day: November 18
Patronage: People who
do not agree with Church authorities

Text by Barbara Yoffie
Illustrated by Katherine A. Borgatti

Liguori
ONE LIGUORI DRIVE
LIGUORI MO 63057-9999

Dedication

**To my family:
my parents Jim and Peg,
my husband Bill,
our son Sam and daughter-in-law Erin,
and our precious grandchildren
Ben, Lucas, and Andrew**

**To all the children I have had the privilege of
teaching throughout the years.**

Imprimi Potest:
Harry Grile, CSsR, Provincial
Denver Province, The Redemptorists

Published by Liguori Publications
Liguori, Missouri 63057

To order, call 800-325-9521
www.liguori.org

p ISBN 978-0-7648-2239-1
e ISBN 978-0-7648-2293-3

Liguori Publications, a nonprofit corporation, is an apostolate of The
Redemptorists. To learn more about The Redemptorists, visit Redemptorists.com.

Printed in the United States of America
17 16 15 14 13 / 5 4 3 2 1
First Edition

Dear Parents and Teachers:

Saints and Me! is a series of children's books about saints. Six books make up the first set: *Saints of North America.* In this set, each book tells a thought-provoking story about a heavenly hero.

Saints of North America includes the heroic lives of six saints from the United States, Canada, and Mexico. Saints Kateri Tekakwitha and Elizabeth Ann Seton were both born in the United States. Saint Juan Diego was born in Mexico, and Saint André Bessette was from Canada. European missionaries also came to North America to spread the Catholic faith, making it their home while they worked with people in the New World. Saints Rose Philippine Duchesne and Damien de Veuster were missionary saints.

Through the centuries, saints have always been dear to Catholics, but *why?* In most instances, ordinary people were and are transformed by the life of Jesus and therefore model Christ's life for us. It is our Lord who makes ordinary people extraordinary. As your children come to know the saints, it is our hope that they will come to understand and identify that they, too, are *called to be saints.*

Which saint wanted to work with Native Americans? Who wanted to work with the sick people on the island of Molokai, Hawaii? To which saint did the Virgin Mary appear? Who loved Saint Joseph? Which saint started the first American religious community of women? Do you know which saint is the patron of nature? Find the answers in the *Saints of North America, Saints and Me!* set and help your child identify with the lives of the saints.

Introduce your children or students to the *Saints and Me!* series as they:

—READ about the lives of the saints and are inspired by their stories.

—PRAY to the saints for their intercession.

—CELEBRATE the saints and relate to their lives.

saints of north America

 Kateri Tekakwitha

 Juan Diego

 Rose Philippine
Duchesne

 Damien of Molokai

 Elizabeth Ann Seton

 André Bessette

Belgium

France

Rose Philippine was a little girl with a big dream. She wanted to be a missionary in America. And she wanted to work with Native Americans.

Philippine was born in Grenoble, France, in 1769. The Duchesne family enjoyed the good things in life. Her mother taught her to care about others. "We should help other people," she told her daughter.

Philippine was taught by the Visitation Sisters. She liked history and reading about the saints. The sisters lived a peaceful and prayerful life. Philippine prayed every day. "Dear God, show me how to love and serve you."

At age eighteen she joined the Visitation convent. A war broke out in France and many things changed. Churches and convents were closed. Philippine went home to her family.

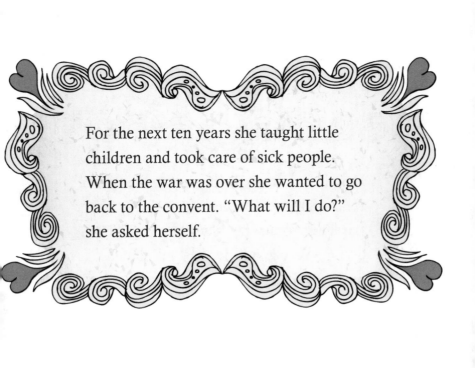

For the next ten years she taught little
children and took care of sick people.
When the war was over she wanted to go
back to the convent. "What will I do?"
she asked herself.

Rose heard about the Society of the Sacred Heart. She met Mother Madeleine Sophie Barat and joined her new convent. They became very good friends. Philippine was now called Sister Philippine.

"I would like to be a missionary in America. I want to work with the Native Americans," she told Mother Barat. Instead, Sister Philippine was sent to Paris, France, to work with the poor.

She still dreamed about going to America. And then one day, her prayers were answered! "The bishop asked for help in America. Who would like to go?" asked Mother Barat. Sister Philippine was the first to say yes!

She and four other sisters left for America. A ship carried them across the wide Atlantic Ocean. The trip was long and difficult. The missionary sisters were happy and excited.

They stepped off the ship in New Orleans and later headed north up the Mississippi River to St. Louis. The bishop sent them to St. Charles where Sister Philippine, now called Mother Duchesne, opened a school.

"We have much to do," she told the other
sisters. Life was very different in the frontier
of America. In the winter it was very cold.
In the summer it was very hot. It was hard
to find food and clean water.

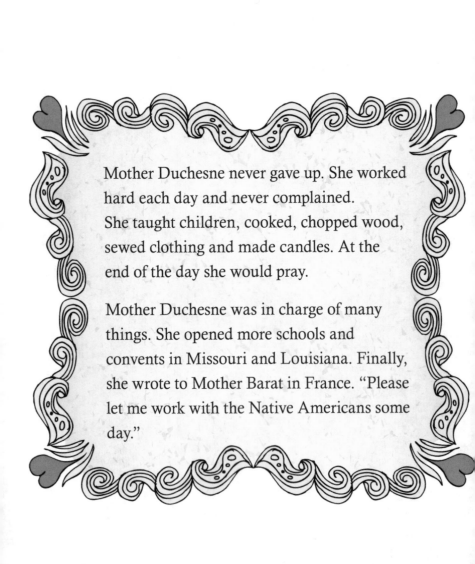

Mother Duchesne never gave up. She worked
hard each day and never complained.
She taught children, cooked, chopped wood,
sewed clothing and made candles. At the
end of the day she would pray.

Mother Duchesne was in charge of many
things. She opened more schools and
convents in Missouri and Louisiana. Finally,
she wrote to Mother Barat in France. "Please
let me work with the Native Americans some
day."

At age seventy-one, she went to Kansas
to work with the Potawatomi Indians!
They loved Mother Duchesne. She prayed for
them day and night. She was sick and weak,
but she loved being with them. They called
her the "Woman Who Prays Always."

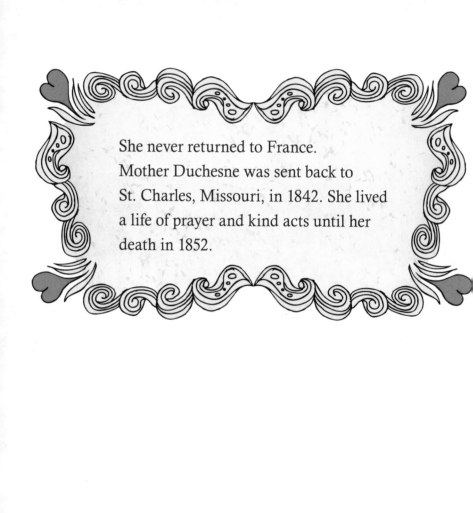

She never returned to France.
Mother Duchesne was sent back to
St. Charles, Missouri, in 1842. She lived
a life of prayer and kind acts until her
death in 1852.

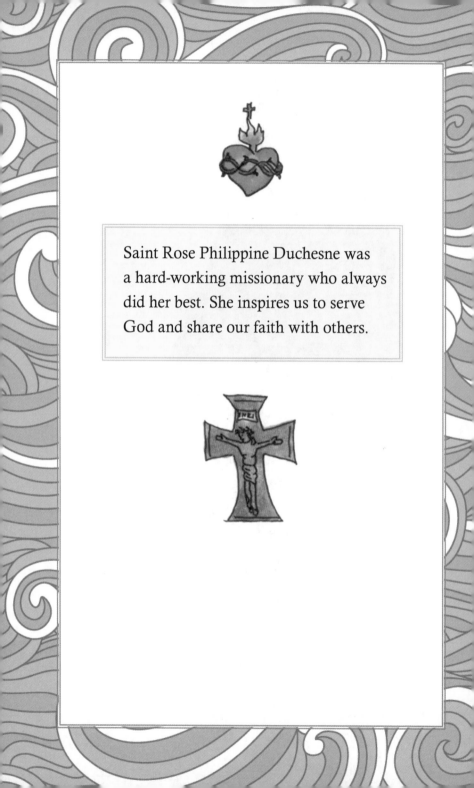

Saint Rose Philippine Duchesne was a hard-working missionary who always did her best. She inspires us to serve God and share our faith with others.

Always hope and always pray.
God will help you through the day.

Dear God,

I love you.

Saint Rose Philippine
loved you with
all her heart.
She liked to pray
all the time.
Help me to grow close
to you when I pray.
Amen.

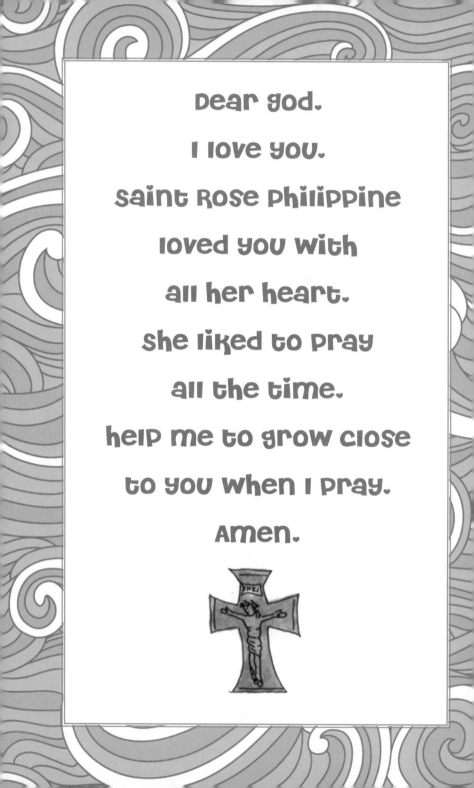

NEW WORDS (Glossary)

Bishop: A priest who is the leader of many churches in a certain area

Convent: A house where a group of women religious live

Frontier: An area of land that has not been explored; wilderness

Missionary: A person who teaches the faith or preaches the gospel in a certain place

Mother: The superior or leader of a group of women religious

Potawatomi Indians: A Native North American tribe that lived in the north central states

Society of the Sacred Heart: A group of women religious founded by Saint Madeleine Sophie Barat in 1800

Visitation Sisters: A group of women religious founded by Saint Francis de Sales and Saint Jane Frances de Chantal in 1610

Rose Philippine's dream was realized as she went on mission. At the Sugar Creek Mission near Centerville, Kansas, she worked with the Potawatomi Indians, who gave her the name "Kwah-kah-kum-ad" (Woman Who Prays Always).